Collins

Easy Learning Maths

Age 5–6

My name is ....

I am .... years old.

I go to .... School.

My birthday is ....

Peter Clarke

How to use this book

- Find a quiet, comfortable place to work, away from other distractions.
- Ask your child what maths they are doing at school and choose an appropriate topic.
- Tackle one topic at a time.
- Help with reading the instructions where necessary, and ensure that your child understands what to do.
- Help and encourage your child to check their own answers as they complete each activity.
- Discuss with your child what they have learnt.
- Let your child return to their favourite pages once they have been completed, to play the games and talk about the activities.
- Reward your child with plenty of praise and encouragement.

Special features

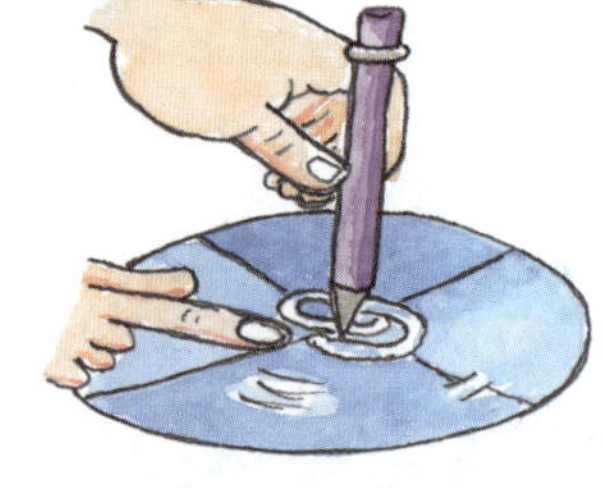

- Games: There is a game on each double page, which reinforces the maths topic. Some of the games require a spinner. This is easily made using a pencil, a paperclip and the circle printed on each games page. Gently flick the paperclip with your finger to make it spin.
- Parent's notes: These are divided into 'What you need to know', which explain the key maths idea, and 'Taking it further', which suggest activities and encourage discussion with your child about what they have learnt. The words in bold are key words that you should focus on when talking to your child.

Published by Collins
An imprint of HarperCollins*Publishers*
77–85 Fulham Palace Road
Hammersmith
London
W6 8JB

Browse the complete Collins catalogue at
www.collins.co.uk

First published in 2006

10 9 8

ISBN 978-0-00-730098-3

British Library Cataloguing in Publication Data
A Catalogue record for this publication is available from the British Library

Written by Peter Clarke
Design and layout by Lodestone Publishing Limited, Uckfield, East Sussex; www.lodestonepublishing.com
Illustrated by Rachel Annie Bridgen;
www.shootingthelight.com
Cover design by Susi Martin
Cover illustration by John Haslam
Printed and bound in China

Contents

Counting to 20

On the farm

- How many of each animal?

☐ horses ☐ dogs ☐ sheep ☐ cows ☐ chickens

Count the spots

- Count the spots. Match the cows.

What you need to know At this stage your child is learning to:

- **count** up to 20 objects, with and without touching them
- recognise that the last number counted refers to the number of objects in the group.

Game: How many?

You need: 1–6 dice, about 50 pasta shapes (or similar).

- Take turns to roll the dice, and pick up that number of shapes.
- After 5 turns each, count how many shapes each person has.
- Who has the most?

Help the farmer!

- The sheep have got mixed up with the cows. How many of each?

☐ sheep ☐ cows

Taking it further Take a handful of e.g. pasta shapes and ask your child to **count** them. Repeat with more/less shapes. Then, put the shapes very close together/spread out/in a line, and ask: 'Is the number still the same?' For groups of less than 10, encourage your child to count without touching each one. Then ask your child to give you e.g. 12 shapes. Repeat for other numbers.

Counting in ones

What number comes next?

- Write the missing numbers.

8 7 6 5 ☐ ☐ ☐

10 11 12 13 14 ☐ ☐ ☐

15 16 17 ☐ ☐ ☐

12 11 10 9 ☐ ☐ ☐

Counting on and back

- What number comes next? 8 9 10 ☐
- Count on 3 from 7. ☐
- Count back 6 from 15. ☐

What you need to know At this stage your child is learning to **count forwards** and **backwards** in **ones**, starting from a small **number**. Being able to count forwards in ones will help your child when they need to add 2 numbers together. (When you are counting forwards together, do not always start at 0 or 1.) Being able to count backwards in ones will help your child when they need to subtract 1 number from another.

Game: Race to the shop!

You need: 1–6 dice, 2 counters.

- Put both counters on My home.
- Take turns to roll the dice. Count forwards the number rolled each time.
- When you get near the shop, work out what number you need to get there.
- Then roll the dice to get home again, this time counting backwards.
- The winner is the first person to reach home.

Dice puzzle

- Roll a 1–6 dice twice. Write down the 2 numbers.

- Count on from the smaller to the larger number.

- Now count back from the larger to the smaller number.

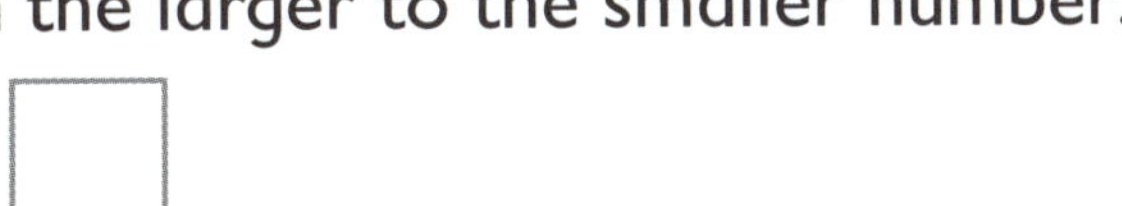

- What do you notice about the number of counts? Why is this?

Taking it further Say a **number** from 0 to 10, e.g. 6. Ask your child to:

- **count forwards** from 6 until you say stop
- **count backwards** from 6 to 0
- **count on** from 6 to 12
- **count back** from 6 to 3
- count on 4 from 6
- count back 5 from 6.

Counting in tens

What number comes next?

- Write the missing numbers.

90 80 70 60

30 40 50

60 50 40

Counting on and back

- What number comes next?

30 40 50 ☐

90 80 70 ☐

- Count on three tens from 30. ☐
- Count back three tens from 70. ☐

What you need to know At this stage your child is learning to **count on** and **back** in steps of 1 and 10, and how to count on in steps of 2, 3 and 5, starting from **zero**, and back again.

Game: Forwards or backwards?

You need: paperclip, pencil, 5 counters (or buttons).

- Put a counter above a number on the number train, e.g. 50. This is your start number.
- Spin the spinner (see page 2).
- Your aim is to land on a coloured carriage. You can count on or back.
- If you land on a coloured carriage, cover the number with a counter.
- The game ends when all the coloured carriages are covered.

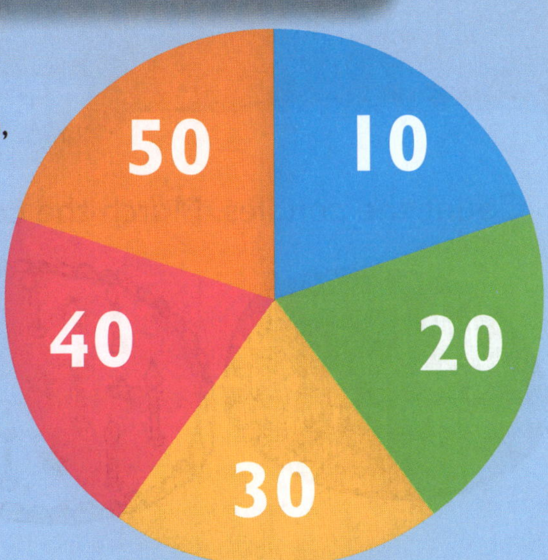

Colour the numbers

- Start at 30. Count on 5 tens. Colour the number red.
- Start at 10. Count on 9 tens. Colour the number blue.
- Start at 50. Count on 1 ten. Colour the number orange.

- Start at 70. Count back 5 tens. Colour the number red.
- Start at 30. Count back 3 tens. Colour the number blue.
- Start at 100. Count back 6 tens. Colour the number orange.

Taking it further Say a multiple of 10 from 10 to 100, e.g. 30, and ask your child to:

- **count forwards** in **tens** from 30 until you say stop
- **count backwards** in tens from 30 to 0
- **count on** from 30 in tens to 80
- **count back** from 60 in tens to 20
- count on 3 tens from 30
- count back 2 tens from 30.

Numbers to 20

Birthday cakes

- Count the candles. Match the cakes.

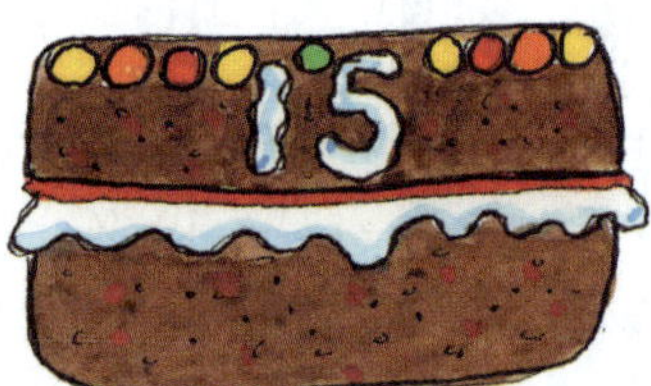

Birthday cards

- Match the cards.

What you need to know At this stage your child is learning to **read** and **write figures** from 0 to 20, and to read and eventually write **words** from **zero** to **twenty**.

Game: Match the numbers

You need: 18 counters.

- One person puts a counter on a number on the present.
- The other person puts a counter on the matching number word.
- Did you both get them all right?

thirteen

ten

five

sixteen

seven

two

fifteen

1 2 5

7 10

15 16

19 20

twelve

nineteen

one

twenty

eight

How many letters?

- Which numbers from 1 to 10 have three letters?

one			

- Which numbers from 1 to 10 have five letters?

- Which numbers from 11 to 20 have eight letters?

Taking it further Using the 'Match the numbers' game, point to a **number** written in **figures** or words. Ask your child to say the number/**read** the **word**. Then ask your child to point to the figures that read: 'seven', 'two', 'sixteen', and the words that read: 5, 12, 19. Go on to say a number (up to 20), and ask your child to **write** it as a **figure**.

Ordering numbers to 20

Number order

- Put the hippos in order.
- Start with the lowest number.

4

Quick quiz

- Write a number between 5 and 10. ☐
- Which of these numbers is the smallest? 15 14 19 ☐

  Which is the largest? ☐
- Say the numbers from 10 to 20, then write 4 numbers that follow one another. ☐

What you need to know Your child needs to be able to order numbers 0 to 20 from **smallest** to **largest**, and largest to smallest. Arranging numbers in **order** and knowing the relative size of numbers in relation to one another is an important skill. (A number line, or number track, will help your child understand number order.)

Game: 4 number run

You need: paperclip, pencil, 2 different coloured pens.

- Take turns to spin the spinner (see page 2).
- Write the number in the right place on the snake number track.
- If the number is already written in, have another go.
- The winner is the person who writes in a number that makes a run of 4 numbers, e.g. 12, 13, 14, 15.

Fill the blanks

- Write a number on each blank elephant so that the numbers are in order.

- Now write different numbers so that the numbers are still in order.

Taking it further Spin the spinner and write down the **number**. Do this 5 times. Ask your child to write the numbers in order from **smallest** to **largest**. Then spin the spinner again, and ask your child to put in the new number so the **order** is still right.

First, second, third

First to last

- Colour the 1st person in the queue red and the 3rd person blue.
- Colour the 7th person green and the 10th person orange.
- Colour the 11th person purple and the last person yellow.

Quick questions

- Which person is before the 2nd person?
- Which people have hats on?
- Point to the 2nd person.
- Is the person in blue third or fourth in line?
- What is the fifth letter of the alphabet?
- How old will you be on your next birthday?

What you need to know Putting things in order (**first**, **second**, etc.) is an important skill for your child to develop, as these numbers are used all the time to order people, objects, time or events.

Game: 6-a-side football

You need: paperclip, pencil, 12 counters (or buttons).

Each person is picking a team to play 6-a-side football.

- Start by putting a counter on each child.
- Take turns to spin the spinner (see page 2). Take a counter off the child that your spin lands on, and keep it.
- If the counter has already gone, miss a turn.
- The winner is the first person to collect 6 players for their team.

Footballs

- Spin the spinner and colour that football.
- Do this 5 times.

   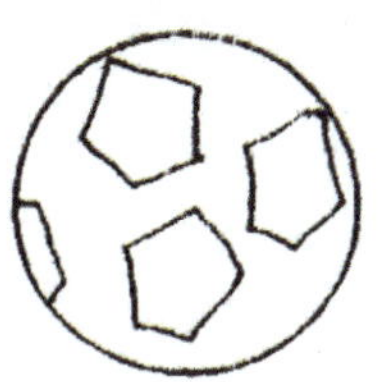  

Taking it further Collect 20 small things from around the home, and put them in a row. Moving from left to right, say: 'This tin is **first** in the line. This spoon is the **second**.' Then ask your child to point to the 3rd/5th/9th/15th… thing. Also ask: 'Where is the banana/spoon/sweet?'

1 or 10 more or less

1 more or less

- Write the number that is 1 more.

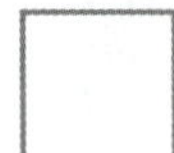
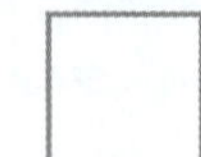

- Write the number that is 1 less.

10 more or less

- Write the number that is 10 more.

- Write the number that is 10 less.

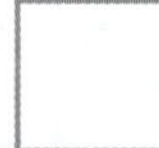

What you need to know Knowing that a number is 1 **more** or 10 **more than** a given number helps your child when they are adding 1 or 10 to a number. Knowing that a number is 1 **less** or 10 **less than** a given number helps when they are subtracting 1 or 10 from a number.

Game: Spinning numbers

You need: paperclip, 2 pencils, paper.

- Write any 6 numbers from 1 to 30.
- Spin the spinner (see page 2).
- Work out 1 more than, 1 less than, 10 more than, and 10 less than the number spun.
- If any of the answers are the 6 numbers you wrote down, cross them out.
- Keep spinning until you have crossed out your 6 numbers.

Missing numbers

- This is part of a 1–100 number grid. Fill in the missing numbers.

	12			15					
21	22	23					28		
	32								

- This is another part of a 1–100 number grid. Fill in the missing numbers.

Taking it further Give your child more practice in working out 1 **more/less** and 10 more/less. Ask: 'What is …1 **more than** 7, …1 **less than** 10, …10 more than 8, …10 less than 13, and 'What number is …1 **after** 11, …1 **before** 6, …10 after 15, …10 before 16?'

Adding numbers to 10

What's the total?

- Use the number track to help you answer these.

3 + 4 = ☐ 5 + 3 = ☐

2 + 7 = ☐ 6 + 0 = ☐

5 + 1 = ☐ 8 + 2 = ☐

4 + 4 = ☐ 3 + 6 = ☐

What do I add?

- Fill in the missing numbers.

☐ + 4 = 6 2 + ☐ = 7

3 + ☐ = 10 ☐ + 2 = 5

4 + ☐ = 9 4 + ☐ = 4

☐ + 7 = 8 2 + ☐ = 3

6 + ☐ = 8 ☐ + 5 = 10

What you need to know At this stage your child is only expected to **add** 2 numbers together to find **totals** up to 10. (A number line, or number track, will help your child to add numbers to 10.)

Game: Addition game

You need: 1–6 dice, 30 counters (or buttons) – 15 of 1 colour, 15 of another.

- Take turns to roll the dice twice. Add the two numbers together.
- Cover that number with one of your counters.
- If you can't find the number, miss a turn.
- The winner is the first person to cover four numbers in a row across, in a column down, or diagonally.

6	12	4	2	3	5
3	5	6	7	11	4
6	2	8	9	5	7
11	5	4	3	6	8
4	3	7	8	4	5
5	7	2	6	10	9

Addition puzzles

- Use the numbers 1, 2 and 3. Make each side of the triangle add up to 5.
- Can you do it another way?

Now try this using the same shape.

- Use the numbers 1, 2, 3, 4, 5 and 6. Make each side of the triangle add up to 10.
- Can you do it another way?

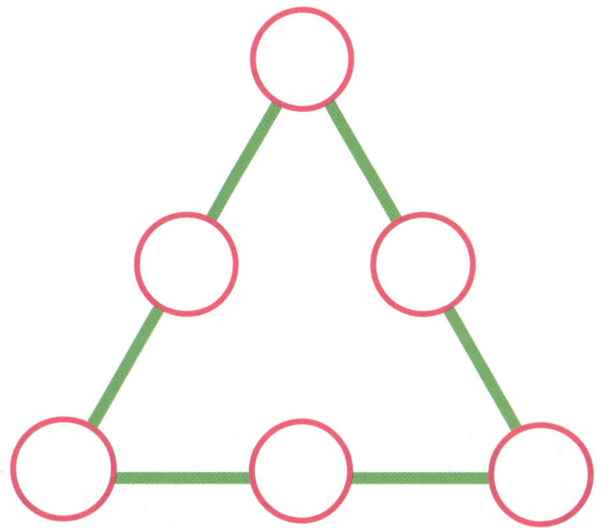

Taking it further Ask your child to count a number of objects, e.g. 5 apples. Ask questions, e.g. '**Add** 2', 'What is 2 **more**?' Encourage your child to remember the larger number, (say: 'Hold the larger number in your head'), and count on the next number, e.g. 5, 6, 7, so 5 add 2 is 7.

Subtracting numbers to 10

How many are left?

- Answer these. Use the number track.

5 – 2 = □	10 – 4 = □
7 – 5 = □	9 – 1 = □
6 – 6 = □	4 – 2 = □
8 – 3 = □	3 – 0 = □

What's missing?

- Answer these. Use the number track.

□ – 3 = 4	7 – □ = 1
9 – □ = 4	□ – 3 = 6
10 – □ = 0	6 – □ = 2
□ – 3 = 2	□ – 5 = 3
□ – 3 = 3	10 – □ = 3

What you need to know At this stage your child is only expected to **subtract** from a number **less than** 10. (Using a number line, or number track, will help your child to subtract numbers to 10.)

Game: Four numbers in a row

You need: paperclip, pencil, 30 counters (or buttons) – 15 of one colour, 15 of another.

- Take turns to spin the spinner (see page 2) twice. Take the smaller number away from the larger number.
- Cover that number with one of your counters.
- If you can't find the number, miss a turn.
- The winner is the first person to cover four numbers in a row across, in a column down, or diagonally.

3	5	1	6	0	2
2	7	8	2	5	0
2	0	3	4	1	9
9	1	6	2	0	1
4	3	0	4	3	6
0	5	7	1	8	4

Subtraction puzzles

- For each puzzle, use the numbers 1, 2, 3, 4 and 5 once only.
- Numbers next to each other must have a difference of more than 1.
- Can you do each puzzle in a different way?

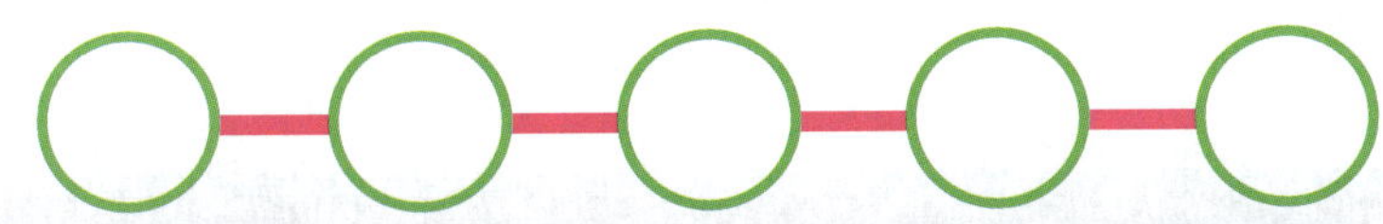

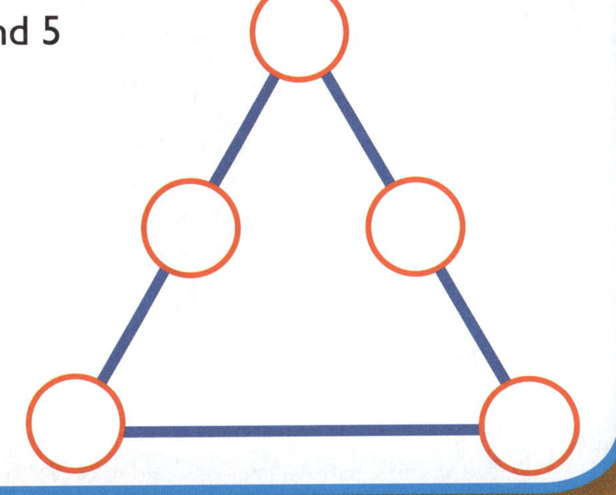

Taking it further Count out 8 counters. Hide 5 of them in a small container. Ask your child to say how many counters they can see, and how many are hidden. Repeat for other numbers.

Making 10

Pairs to make 10

- Join the pairs that have a total of 10 spots.

Pairs to 10

- Write the other number to make 10.

What you need to know Your child should know by heart all pairs of numbers that make 10, e.g. 0 + 10, 1 + 9, 2 + 8, 3 + 7, 4 + 6, 5 + 5. This will help when they come to adding pairs of numbers where the answer is greater than 10, e.g. 8 + 5 = 8 + 2 + 3 = 10 + 3 = 13.

Game: How many more?

You need: paperclip, pencil, 20 counters (or buttons) – 10 of 1 colour, 10 of another.

- Spin the spinner (see page 2).
- How many more to make 10?
- Find that snail. Cover the number with a counter.
- If you can't find the number, miss a turn.
- The winner is the person with the most counters when all the numbers are covered.

Same total puzzles

- Use these numbers to make the same total in each circle.
  2 3 4 5 6
- You can only write each number once.

- Use these numbers. 1 2 3 4
- Make each row across, column down, and diagonal of 4 numbers total 10.

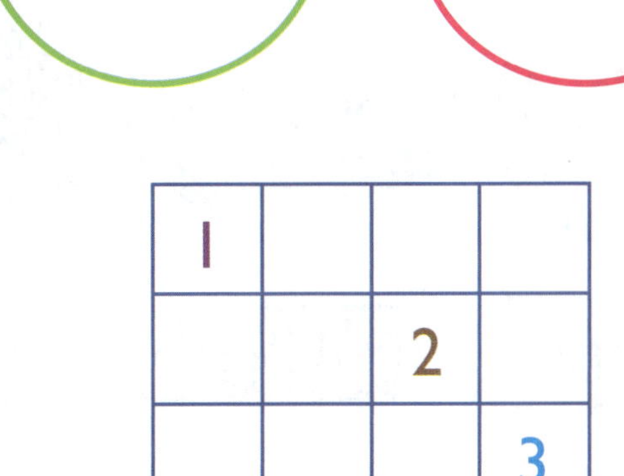

Taking it further Spin the spinner. If it lands on e.g. 6, ask: '**How many more** do you need to **add** to 6 to make 10?' Repeat several times. Then ask: 'Tell me 2 numbers that have a **total** of 10. Can you tell me another pair? Are there any others?

Money

Counting money

- How much money is in each purse?

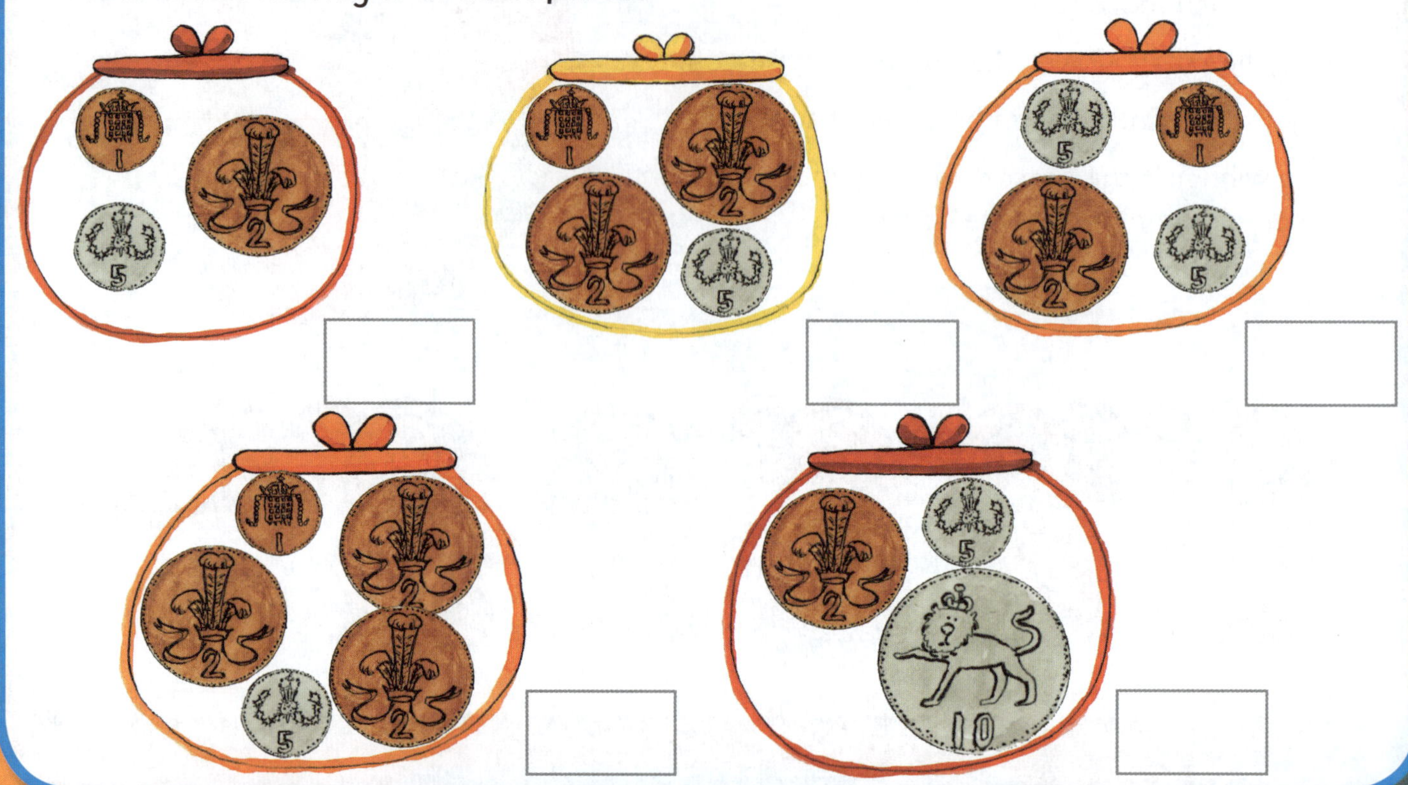

Change

- How much change would you get from 20p?

What you need to know At this stage your child is learning to **add** the **total** of 2 or more items up to 20p, and give **change** to 20p. When calculating change, encourage your child to count up from the total to the amount of **money** offered, e.g. for items costing 14p when 20p is offered: count on from 14p to 20p. (A number line, or number track, is useful for showing this.)

Game: Money game

You need: paperclip, pencil, paper, 10 counters (or buttons).

- Spin the spinner (see page 2) twice.
- Add the amounts and say the total.
- Find some food for that price.
- Put a counter on the price ticket.

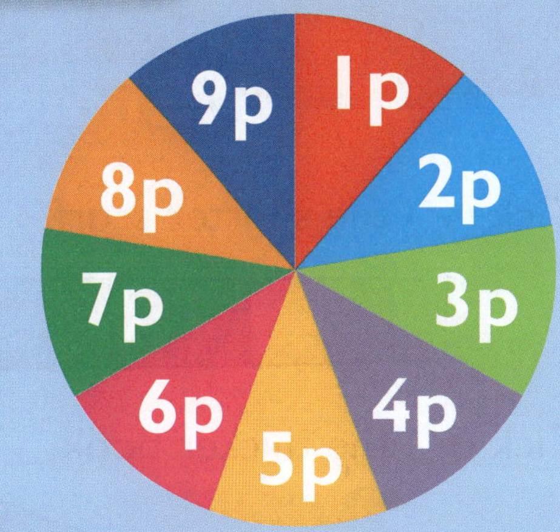

Using money

- What different amounts can you make using 2 of these coins?

- How much change would you get from 20p if you spent each of these amounts?

Taking it further Spin the spinner 2 or 3 times and ask your child to say how much it is in **total**. Then ask: 'If I bought something in a shop worth 14p and I gave the shopkeeper 20p, **how much change** would I get?'

Comparing measures

Shorter, thicker, tallest

- Tick (✔) the shorter scarf.

- Tick (✔) the thicker book.

- Tick (✔) the tallest child.

Lightest, heavier, more, half full

- Tick (✔) the lightest animal.

- Tick (✔) the heavier bag.

- Tick (✔) the jug that holds more.

- Tick (✔) the glass that is half full.

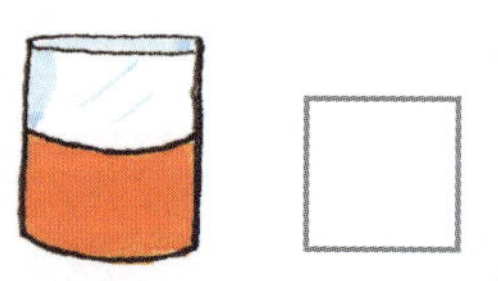

What you need to know At this stage your child is comparing 2 **lengths**, **widths**, **heights**, **depths**, **weights** and **capacities** (**shorter**, **thicker** etc.) and then comparing more than 2 (**tallest**, **lightest** etc.).

Game: The length game

You need: paperclip, pencil, 12 counters (or buttons).

- Take turns to spin the spinner (see page 2).
- Put the word into a sentence to describe one of the pairs, e.g. This car is shorter than that car.
- If you are right, take a counter.
- The winner is the first person to collect 6 counters.

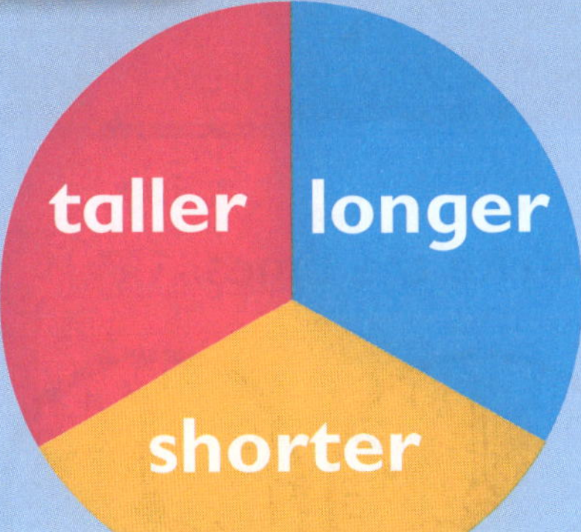

Can you find...?

- Look around your home to find these things.

Taking it further Choose several different-sized packets or tins from the kitchen cupboard. Ask your child to hold one in each hand and to tell you which is **lighter**. They keep the lighter one each time until they have found the **lightest** item. Try again for length, finding the **longest/shortest** item. Then repeat for **capacity**, finding the container that holds the **most/least** amount of water.

Time

Telling the time

- Write the times.

What's the time?

- Draw the times.

9 o'clock

1 o'clock

half past 3

half past 5

2 o'clock

half past 8

What you need to know At this stage your child is learning to: understand and use words related to **time**; order familiar events in time; know the days of the **week**/seasons of the **year**; read the time to the **hour** or **half hour** on **clock** faces.

Game: Yes or No?

- One person thinks of a time, day of the week, or season.
- The other person tries to guess that time by asking questions that have a 'Yes' or 'No' answer.
- Count how many questions you ask before you guess the time.

o'clock

half past

season

day of the week

morning

afternoon

night

What happens when?

- What do you do on a Monday? Draw a picture.
- What do you do in the Summer? Draw a picture.
- What do you do at 1 o'clock? Draw a picture.

Taking it further When the **clock** shows an o'clock or half past time, ask your child what **time** it is. Also, what time it was an **hour** ago, in an hour's time, and in half an hour's time. Using your holiday photos, ask your child questions related to time, e.g. 'When did we go to…? Was it yesterday/last week/winter?'

Shapes

Flat shapes

- Match the shape to its name.

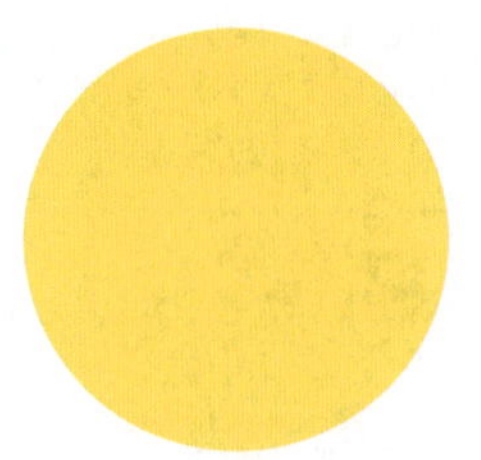

square

triangle

rectangle

circle

Solid shapes

- Match the shape to its name.

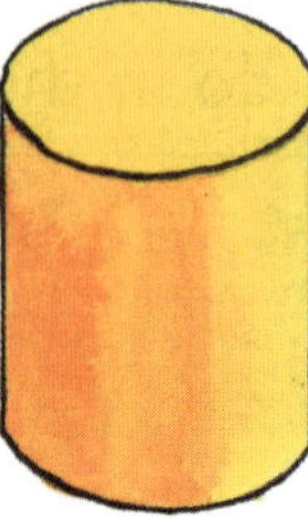

cuboid

cone

sphere

cylinder

cube

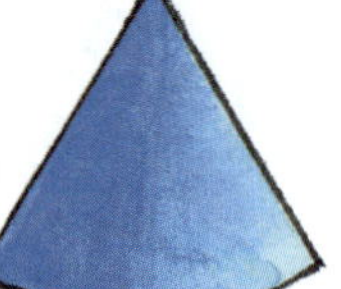

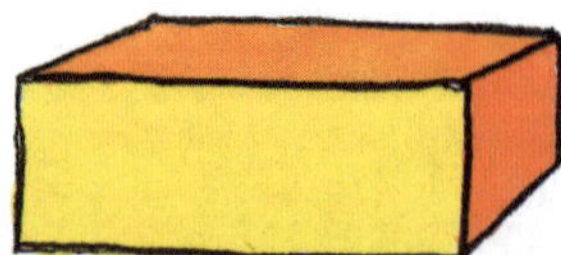

What you need to know At this stage your child is learning to:

- recognise and name simple **flat (2D) shapes**, e.g. **circle**, **triangle**, **square**, **rectangle**, and to count the number of **sides** and **corners** each shape has.
- recognise and name simple **solid (3D)** shapes, e.g. **cube**, **cuboid**, **sphere**, **cone**, **cylinder**, and to count the number of **faces**, **edges** and corners each shape has.

Game: Shapes

You need: paperclip, pencil.

- Spin the spinner (see page 2).
- Can you name a shape that has that number of sides, faces or corners?

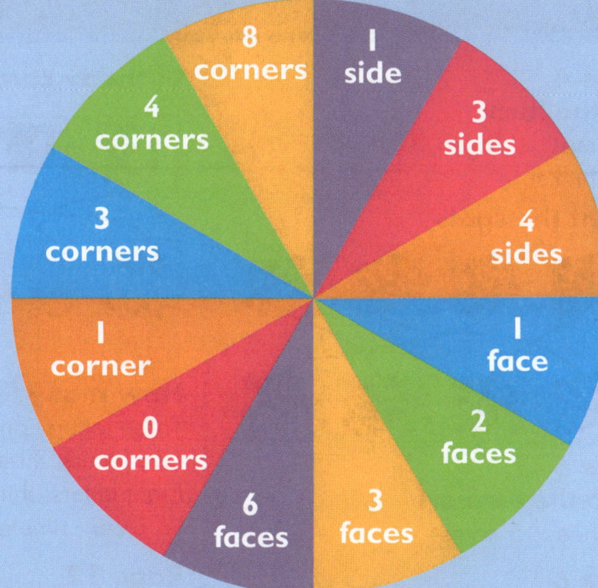

Same shapes

- What things are round like this coin?

- What things are cubes like this dice?

Taking it further At home, or when you are out, look at different **shapes**. Ask: 'What shape is this plate/mirror/bathmat/tea-towel/window/door/the green traffic light'? Choose a shape for the week, e.g. a **circle**. How many of these shapes can your child spot?

Answers

Page 4

On the farm

4 horses, 3 dogs, 12 sheep, 7 cows, 16 chickens

Count the spots

Page 5

Help the farmer!

13 sheep, 5 cows

Page 6

What number comes next?

8, 7, 6, 5, 4, 3, 2
10, 11, 12, 13, 14, 15, 16, 17
15, 16, 17, 18, 19, 20
12, 11, 10, 9, 8, 7, 6

Counting on and back

8, 9, 10, 11
3 on from 7 = 10
6 back from 15 = 9

Page 7

Dice puzzle

Check your child's answers.
The number of counts is the same because the numbers you are counting on and back from are the same.

Page 8

What number comes next?

90, 80, 70, 60, 50, 40, 30, 20
30, 40, 50, 60, 70, 80, 90
60, 50, 40, 30, 20, 10

Counting on and back

30, 40, 50, 60
90, 80, 70, 60
three tens on from 30 = 60
three tens back from 70 = 40

Page 9

Colour the numbers

Page 10

Birthday cakes

Birthday cards

Page 11

How many letters?

Three letters: one, two, six, ten
Five letters: three, seven, eight
Eight letters: thirteen, fourteen, eighteen, nineteen

Page 12

Number order

4, 5, 6, 7, 8, 9
6, 7, 12, 17, 18, 20
2, 3, 10, 11, 13, 16

Quick quiz

Number between 5 and 10 = 6, 7, 8 or 9
Smallest number = 14
Largest = 19
Check that your child has written 4 numbers that follow one another.

Page 13

Fill in the blanks

6 different answers are possible:
8, 9, 12, 13, 15
8, 9, 12, 14, 15
8, 10, 12, 13, 15
8, 10, 12, 14, 15
8, 11, 12, 13, 15
8, 11, 12, 14, 15

Page 14

First to last

Quick questions

The 1st and 11th people have hats on.

The person in blue is 3rd.
The fifth letter of the alphabet is the letter e.
Check your child answers the question correctly.

Page 15

Footballs

Check your child's answers.

Page 16

1 more or less

1 more: 3, 9, 17, 14
1 less: 4, 6, 0, 17

10 more or less

10 more: 13, 16, 18, 20
10 less: 4, 7, 1, 9

Page 17

Missing numbers

				5					
	12		14	15	16		18		
21	22	23		25		27	28	29	
	32						38		

		3						9	
	12	13	14		16		18	19	20
		23		25	26	27		29	
					36				

Page 18

What's the total?

3 + 4 = 7
2 + 7 = 9
5 + 1 = 6
4 + 4 = 8

5 + 3 = 8
6 + 0 = 6
8 + 2 = 10
3 + 6 = 9

What do I add?

2 + 4 = 6
3 + 7 = 10
4 + 5 = 9
1 + 7 = 8
6 + 2 = 8

2 + 5 = 7
3 + 2 = 5
4 + 0 = 4
2 + 1 = 3
5 + 5 = 10

Page 19

Addition puzzle

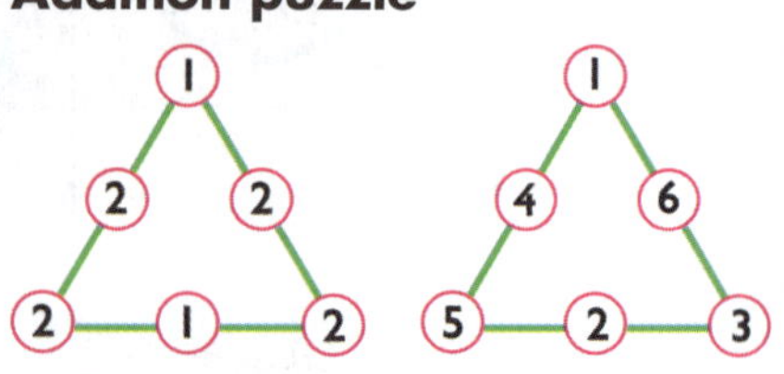

Other answers are possible.